WINTER WORK

Peter Fallon

Winter Work

 Gallery Books

Winter Work
is published simultaneously
in paperback and in a
clothbound edition in March 1983.

The Gallery Press
19 Oakdown Road
Dublin 14. Ireland.

ISBN 0 904011 35 6 (clothbound)
     0 904011 36 4 (paperback)

The Gallery Press receives financial assistance from The Arts
Council/An Chomhairle Ealaíon, Ireland.

Contents

Acknowledgements

The author acknowledges the help of The Arts Council/An Chomhairle Ealaíon, Ireland, by way of a bursary in 1981, in the writing of these poems. Acknowledgements are due to the editors and publishers of *The Connacht Tribune* (*Writing in the West*), *Feathers and Bones* (California), *The First Ten Years: Dublin Arts Festival Poetry, Hibernia, The Irish Press* (*New Irish Writing*), *The Irish Times, Pequod* (California), Pinchpenny Press (Indiana), *Poetry Ireland Review, Poetry Review* (London), *Quarryman, Sunday Independent* (*Poem of the Month*), *Times Literary Supplement, Young Poets from Ireland* (Blackstaff Press) and *The Writers: A Sense of Ireland* (O'Brien Press/George Braziller, New York) in which some of these poems were published first.

Notes

p. 40 *Bhfuil cead agam dul amach:* May I leave the room?

p. 45 *céilí:* a friendly visit, social call.

p. 48 *meitheal:* a co-operative work force.

Home

for Paul Muldoon

The faraway hills are green but these
are greener. My brother roamed the world
and seemed to know everything. He boasted it
until I burst, 'Well you don't know John Joe Farrell',

the butcher's son, my friend. I balanced all beside
a field in County Meath, its crooked acres falling
south. We called a hill *Sliabh na Cailli,* the hag's mountain,
but that's the way it is for lowlanders will call

a small incline a mountain and mountain-men mention
a hill and point to Everest. Things were themselves.
We bore them as the Cuckoo Clarke bore his origin,
humbled, naturally. We were masters of reserve.

'Why?' 'That's the way.' 'Ah why?' 'Because . . .'
When all fruit fails we welcome haws.

Faith

When we were young and visiting
there were in every house
the nails that nailed Jesus,
the Saviour, to the Cross.

They lay in inlaid cabinets
with photographs and delph
and sometimes by the relics
of some old saint himself.

We called their rust the rust
of blood and learned
of sacrifice. We said they were
the real nails although we knew they weren't.

Loughcrew

They say, I've always heard,
there's not a lake in County Meath.
The width or breadth of it
no river swells or springs collect.
I'm living in the townland of Loughcrew,
loch na craoibhe, lake of the limb
of the oak on the island.

I wasn't born here but I came
to be at home near my home place.
I'm looking at the maps
and see the lake, a boat-house,
trees in Traynors' field,
a pair of islands. Now there's one.

They say that I say little,
say I fish in deeper waters.
An island is lost, a lake is found
and I translate an early verse:
  'I am the poor hag of Bera.
  Many a wonder have I seen.
  I have seen Carnbawn a lake
  Although it's now a mountain green.'

Cailleach

for Eilís O'Connell

1
Whose children were tribes
and races? *The hag's.*
Whose lovers were heroes
and gods? *The hag's.*
Who hails from Loughcrew?

Maiden and crone,
sister and bride of the sun,
shape-shifter, mist-eater,
scarcely seen;

beldame of the hazels,
haunter of heather,
maker of mountains,
mother of magic:

Grant a fair wind.

2
Who hides in the last
swath to be reaped?
Who stays in the last
stook to be tied?

Who turned to stone
the men on guard
around Sliabh na Caillí?

She whose name the mountain took,
who went to the lake to drink,
from whom the ragged weeds of age
have fallen seven times,

who's kind to the plough,
who danced through stumbling-blocks,
who wears a nun's veil now.

The Mass-hour

We knew the land preserved
and presumed the fattest game,
and knew the Master's habit
of Mass, and waited. Out he came

and in we went. We trod
along a marshy ditch,
flushed pigeons, ducks,
like small grenades. The bitch

began to set and we to aim.
The time she gave we might
have been out shooting clays
and calling to the trap-man 'Right',

we were so well prepared.
Cock pheasants rose and fell.
We tramped as if we owned the place,
close enough to smell

the dunghill, down by the backs
of slated sheds, long loose-boxes,
rising snipe and plover,
attentive to the musk of randy foxes,

and then to other land, the hour
up, across to Peadar's Wood
and set again and wounded one
which was retrieved while we stood

stuck midstream. By plough-
and pasturelands, treading hedgerows,
we tracked the prints of game
and kept within the shadows,

men drawn to the chase,
catch and kill, encroachers
on forbidden fields, encouraged by
one cognisance: 'Good keepers tempt good poachers'.

We struck, Ronan, Thosh and I,
as if the saints approved.
The dog did well, the bag grew full,
and then the whole world moved —

we were walking on water,
the skin of a bog.
The way we were killing
we might have been gods.

The Lost Field

for Tanya and Wendell Berry

Somewhere near Kells in County Meath
a field is lost, neglected, let by common law.

When the Horse Tobin went to the bad
and sold a farm and drank the money
there was outlying land we couldn't find.

The maps weren't marked.
My people farmed the farm.
They looked and asked about.
They kept an ear to the ground.

They asked the Horse himself.
He handed out handfuls of fivers,
cups of whiskey, and sang dumb.

When I came home from Dublin
I found my place.
My part in this is reverence.

Think of all that lasts. Think of land.
The things you could do with a field.
Plough, pasture or re-claim. The stones
you'd pick, the house you'd build.

Don't mind the kind of land,
a mess of nettles even
for only good land will grow nettles.
I knew a man shy from a farm
who couldn't find a weed
to tie the pony to.

Imagine the world
the place your own windfalls could fall.

I'm out to find that field, to make it mine.

Acts of Restoration

One day I watched my cousins work
in ways they'd learned
since I left Lennoxbrook
for boarding school, the years
at university. They handled
new machines with ease and undertook

without delay endeavours which to us
were Eden, enticing but forbidden,
and soon I turned
towards remembered haunts and rummaged
in the barn, the passage sheds,
up in the loft. Then time adjourned

among the relics of the work
and play I'd grown on—
the churn, the earthen crocks,
the small milk cans and milking stool,
a weather vane the big wind knocked
in 1961, a coulter, socks,

the cobwebbed harness for the team,
collar, hames and britching,
bit and winkers,
a long rein rope,
a gallon jar, the head
of a pick, and pots awaiting tinkers.

A cap hung on a hook. Doors
leaned against a wall calling
to be opened—and I began
an act of restoration
and matched again
the implements to the man

or beast who wielded them,
the plough to Pat,
the whiskey jar to Joe,
the hardened harness to the horses,
this to that,
those to others so

a world was remedied
and lightened by the articles
of leisure—a croquet set,
striped deck-chairs slumped
like old awnings, a sleigh,
a tricycle, a tennis net—

for as they worked they played,
the earnest labourers
of Lennoxbrook.
I've heard men tell and love to tell
about a year December weather
stayed and shook

ripe crops and long acres
though no sun shone
to make them hay or harvest.
The townland tired of Winter.
Grandfather mowed a single strip
the first day blessed

by blue and started Sports,
held races for the neighbours
and each incomer
to the place. It rained again
that night, the sheds unstacked,
but they'd their summer.

21

The same man looked another day
and dreamed a tennis court
where grass sloped
to the pond. He called the men
from hoe- and harrowing
to level lawns. They roped

a mare to roots and pulled.
They stretched a net and painted lines,
sent invitations countrywide.
Not all was play but all
was happy.
We worked with animals that died

and still a herd evolved.
The months defined the time
for breaking ground and sowings,
for witherings and reaping.
We were at home,
we knew our place between comings and goings.

Fostering

He was lost in the blizzard of himself
and lay, a cold white thing, in a drift
of afterbirth. Another stood to drink dry spins.
I put him with the foster ewe who sniffed

and butted him from his birthright, her milk.
I took the stillborn lamb and cleft
with axe on chopping-block its head,
four legs, and worked the skin apart with deft

skill and rough strength. I dressed the living lamb
in it. It stumbled with the weight, all pluck,
towards the ewe who sniffed and smelled and licked
raiment she recognised. Then she gave suck—

and he was Esau's brother and I was Isaac's wife
working kind betrayals in a field blessed for life.

Gravities

7 *Stillborn*
Some warped, a loss mid-term.
Some spilled daft lambs, a twin
that trailed its fellow and fell to fox
or crow.
          And she delivered perfectly
triplets that nestled in the womb
like seeds five months in earth
expecting a nativity and now are licked
as love might lick a stone.

They stilled an almost human cry and died
the other side of death, died still to be born.

8 *Water-dogs*
They're either sheep- or water-dogs:
if they don't take to work, they're put
to water, tied in a sack. Not worth feeding.
Some herd well and wander still.

They stray to kill and when they kill
they're seldom seen; they never harm their care—
water-dogs, for blooded dogs will wash,
will wade the streams of guilt.
                              Caught,
they're put to water, rounding fishes,
long sleep and dreams of cold-blooded killings.

9 *Nativity*
She kept a compact since tup-time,
the cross-bred hogget in the shed.
She sprang proud teats
and grew a bellows in the belly
to heave and shove against defeat.

I reached to help. My seeing fingers
turned a couple in the womb.
I pulled by front feet, held by hind
until they breathed. Cords and cleanings
dangled; the lambs, the lambs stood up.

10 *Shearing*
Culled for clipping, hoggets and crones,
prodded from fields to folds, from lambs—
the pens are loud with loss.
                                        Late May,
a whir like flies is Padraic
tethered to a plug, smothered in sweat.
He shears, treats rot, pares feet,
and brands.
                    The wool's rolled
like a sleeping-bag, the sheep released
one by one. They line a ridge like Indians,
circling, suspicious, entirely fleeced.

The Hares

for Marie and Seamus

Look out into the garden.
There's nothing there. Clap hands—
a dimpled shadow stands to attention,
stares at the front door,
and you'd need them all, my friend,
your names for the hare,
to put a name on each of these
you'd need them all and more

besides. For eight weeks now
the coursing club has combed the countryside
and gathered them on Sundays,
odd fish they ran aground in trawls
they'd fixed in open fields,
and hauled in husks to be a school.
They freed them to an other life
behind this high walled garden's walls.

Stand out there
and listen to the drumming of their feet,
the shared heartbeat of warning,
for now they're worried witless.
Watch them go, off again,
obliging with their slanting arcs,
the rough freehand of circling runs,
and be the privileged witness

to the nibbled windbreaks of their forms,
their weathered paths nowhere
in the grass, crooked paths
such as sheep and cattle roam

to water or a gate, but here's no open gate
and here they drink dew from morning grass,
sup rain. They are eating themselves
out of house and home.

When I was young I let them go one night
the night before the races.
I think it settled nothing. Now torn between
friends and sympathies my best is second-best:
for months I've fed them every night,
left oats and carrots under pines,
away from crows. They've only left
their brown eggs in a swollen nest.

They'll soon be run down bottle-necks,
lanes of hessian, netting-wire.
Their safe-houses aren't safe.
They'll bite. They'll make shrill sounds
like birds, like babies. They will be transported
to the track, trained to course, to run
for their lives from the perfect pistons
of black and white and brindled hounds.

Moons

By the light of the harvest moon
the combine-harvester whose wheel
made of hill fields a Mississippi
paddled through the waving acres
to dock beside the shearing-shed.
We dried the grain and packed the barns,
stacked bales of oat- and barley-straw,
and McNamees let out the stubble geese.

By the light of the hunter's moon
as first frost fell and sloes bulged
like cows' eyes, the sounds of night
were sounds of foxes, nesting fowl,
reviving rivers, and we prepared.
We killed to eat or killed to purge
and I condemned the useless slaughter,
the gadgets used to draw the pelts.

I was driving home one night
and caught in my headlights a sundered pair
of badgers, a sow that moved, a boar
that didn't. She had lingered nearby
shuffling in bushes, quietly keening,
and nudged to remind the body be well.
Could she have travelled across
from the other world, this widow who scuffed

the beaten path through moonlight,
could she have come all these years on,
mumbling her music, her ancient warning?
I reached to touch the stiffening back
as after argument one would a lover
or as I reached to touch my father lying
late that morning turned towards the wall.
My shyness was fear, fear that he'd turn

on me again. I was afraid until I saw
the bruised blood stopped in his elbow.
I lay the badger in the ditch and looked
for her who trod both lights. She was nowhere
to be seen. She was leading me on,
leading me down the long halls of her sett,
bringing me back. A moon shone brightly
in front of me. There was home in its eclipse.

The County Home

1

They were born in the other century,
almost all of them, and several are over
a hundred years old. Parnell was alive,
a Member for Meath. Theirs was the future,

the road they were on.
Tom Tighe sits smoking, handsome,
calm. He tells of far fair days,
days off school. He would rather be home

walking the miles to Point to Points, talking
to friends. 'I'd crawl on my hands and knees',
he smiles, his last leg propped on a stool,
all the time in the world for taking his ease.

2

Della Kelly, her name is music, Della Kelly,
a sight for sore eyes, a treat to behold
with her mother's crochet draped on her shoulders,
names for the nurses and a look that is bold

as she talks of the warmth, the care and comfort
and food you wouldn't get in a hotel.
Four bands and the Wren Boys came in at Christmas
and singled her out, she danced her fill.

3

There's no sleep at all for Paddy McElarney
and there's nothing to say to a man
who is tied to a chair in the County Home,
who breaks down

and cries, 'Will I ever get home,
ever get home to my own place?
Will I ever be let walk again
the towpath by my little house?'

There is nothing to say, and we say 'Yes'.
'Yes', we lie, 'when the weather's right'.
He cries again and then repeats,
'There's no sleep at all at night'.

'Do you know where you are, Paddy?'
'I do and I'll tell.' He names a place
thirty miles from where we are.
He is thinking of the Workhouse,

doting. He must go to the funeral
of one long dead.
He was out on the town early that day . . .
He glimpses his life through the bars of his bed.

The Conny Ward

By name and nature Conny Ward.

His father knew the faction fights
and saw evictions in the Famine
and he stole land in de Valera's time.
He moved the marks in dark of night.

These men from cottages and cabins,
of poaching and poitín,
they are the true heroes:
their sovereign thought was Ireland.

They toiled and thrifted and had
much ado, took travelling trades
and hurried home, and Tom Ward bested
each of them, their friends and faraways.

They fought the Black and Tans
and wintered in damp ditches.
Without their kind there'd not be
a Republic. They saw the sheep and cattle

maimed. 'That was the worst,
to hear the innocents in pain.'
And saw less meals than mealtimes.
Now they remember well and wish

they could forget, unlettered men
who studied tales while harrowing
and told to file away the nights.
When Conny spoke you'd stand

in snow to listen, so still
you'd hear grass grow. He'd tell all
from the root to bloom, hatfuls of things
to mind today and all tomorrows,

and now he's in the hospital
and made wear silly spectacles.
He's 94. The spiders of age
have woven grey webs in his hair.

The eyes that spotted Granard Spire
know visitors by voices.
Still 'you're a great man, Tom'.
'I was. I was.'

Catholics

The man at the bar is cursing women;
he hates his wife and loves his mother
and tells who'll hear of the whores
he's ridden. When they hadn't a woman
they improvised, himself and another,

behind the ballrooms of their need
they actualised their monstrous art
and in the dark they dreamt of Mary.
And maybe I'm as bad—
I've come for the loan of an ass and cart

and listen to deeds at the Parish Sports
that gorged a greed that knew no bounds.
'Sports is right! That woman's a mother
in England now.' And he escaped. He ran
with the hare and chased with the hounds.

I'm enjoying the stout and the others' talk
but he badgers me,
'We'll have a big night out, both of us,
we'll travel far and find a pair
and none will know, there'll be nobody

the wiser'. And I say 'Aye'
and turn the talk to the ass's age,
her use for foddering, and mention
rain and local news—a death, a sale,
a harvest saved—but he has me in a cage

and starts up again,
'Are you married yourself, *a mhic*?'
'I was never asked.'
'Sure you've maybe no need, you've maybe
a woman who'll do the trick.'

'You know how it is . . .'
I give nothing away, driftwood
on the tide of his surmise
my answer. But I need the ass
and only say 'Be good to that good

woman of yours' though I think to myself
'May your young possess her quality'.
We settle a plan to collect the cart.
He's drunk and I'm linked by one request,
teasing his yes, fending our complicity.

Winter Stores

1 *Bullocks*
They were bred to this since first they burst
upon the scene of stone shed floors
and stood to sample powdered milk.
In cattle crushes they were changed,
skulled and squeezed. Sons of bulls,
they'll never be their fathers' sons.

They drive the wedges of their heads
to feed and fatten, but only hold their own
until new grass. As dragons breathed fire
they breathe hay's burning memories,
a cloud that lingers like lichen,
that could cast a shadow.

Bred to this, they're thick-skinned and offended—
the clips in their ears, their two black eyes.

2 *Heifers*
We called it 'a-bulling', said one was 'away'
or 'noticed' one morning traipsing the track
into the byre. They'd jump the moon
or, worse, a ditch—blood on the barbs
of thorn and wire. They'd mount each other
uselessly.
       But these are dull,
that winter in the yard, that sit
and face the rain or slouch around
as though they were tethered to the hay.
More than daughters, not yet mothers,
the middle breed, in mud and muck,
the mild mortar of next year's field,

they gaze across a five-bar gate
to where the grass conceives a growth.

Ewes

They follow the herdhorse to fodder in snow
and stir to unstitch the woof and warp
of sward in May. They summer
on high lands and winter on low,
stars in a green sky, hundreds of ewes.

I walk one way and they another,
toward and round me, surging to swell
a panic I began behind me. Gathered
like midges, they brace to brave all weathers
and settle down to gimmering, to being mothers.

Sabbath

Just before Christmas, after frost,
the year's best winter morning,
I've tended to the household chores—
lit the fires, fed the fowl,
boiled shirts and towels,
done the dishes, swept the floors.

I cross the fields to friends.
Quite by instinct now
I follow in a herd's
footsteps and look for what
I hope I will not find. Talk
of the devil, name a weed . . . her turds

tell that this ewe lay overnight
and maybe much of yesterday
stuck in the mud
of frozen furrows. I lift
and hold her, walking her in circles
to circulate the blood.

She stumbles and she falls.
Try again, she falls again.
I rub her legs, she falls
again. Still I massage, talking
to her all the while.
I let go and she sprawls.

Of all the herd I can recall
her lambing, and finally I fetch
the transport-box and tractor
and bring her to the long road shed
where her first lamb had stumbled,
fallen, and begun to walk, an actor

on the boards, rehearsing his first
starring role. Then all it took
was time and a will. The night
comes on. She lies in straw.
I leave her water, hay, crushed oats.
If she begins to eat she'll be all right.

And trudge homeward again
across the cross-ploughed fields.
Home again—there's trouble at the door.
The darkness drowns the shortest day.
I sit by blazing firelight
and calculate the cure.

Bill

Booted in Winter, barefoot in Spring,
the scholars trudged along the road
with firesticks and sods of turf,
tea in bottles, cuts of bread.

The first to smoke was Bill,
first to curse. He'd mitch or else
be late and have excuses,
'There's frost our way, there's such ice

on the road would make a body take
one step forward, two steps
back'. 'Then how did you arrive at all?'
the clever master's quip.

'By giving up,
by turning to go home.'
Bill didn't care for copybook or compass
'I was five years at a poem.

I could still recite the start of it . . .
My only Irish ever was *Bhfuil
cead agam dul amach'*
to smoke Woodbines, to play handball.

He liked Geography—
it showed the places he might go.
The winners at Navan or the Park
were all he ever craved to know.

At last he built to marry
and leave his sister on her own
but *she* upped and married
their friend, John.

Bill drank away both work and wife.
With two houses he's on his own
who'd one home and two women.
Then we got great with one

another, Bill and I, visited and talked.
We walked the river after dark,
we hunted here, went racing there;
he brought me my first fighting-cock.

I drink a pint, he minerals or Moussy.
'Sure they're themselves', someone murmurs.
We carry on easily, landlords
of the long acre, sky-farmers.

We know the way it is. We live
our lives; things happen. We know
the worth of the world
to a man when his wife is a widow.

The Heart of Ireland

Late evening in late Spring,
I saddle myself to spray
docks and nettles, a day's work done.
I could be playing a set of pipes,
pumping bellows beneath my elbow.
Late birds add grace notes to the drone.

I work at my slow walking pace,
loving the labour, and find myself begin
—lost in a rhythm—to backpack
into memory: twenty years ago
I stumbled underneath the weight
of bluestone in a brown knapsack

when the men were resting, looking on;
and backtrack further
to the far end of those drills,
to the heart of Ireland,
a stain of blight, stench on the wind,
rotten stalks and tubers, spent chlorophylls.

We strained against an end of faith
in God, toward a field
of solid fruit and flowers,
and woke with proud relief
the day the furrows glowed
as if, overnight, showers

of snow had come to stay or flocks
of white butterflies had lit along the rows.
Late evening in late Spring I'm rounding
up the weeds for grass to grow.
The nights are bright till after ten.
I work till after dark busking

away to my heart's content, and I recall
a famine carried on the wind.
Beyond the garden wall a breeze
begins to blow. The centre strains
to hold. A half-moon tilts between
dead ash- and old apple-trees.

Confederates

The old ones by the fireside
indent their pensions on hot halves
and launch the week-end in Phil Reilly's.
At dinner time workmen come in and suddenly
it's their half-day. Girls come home
from jobs in Dublin, new Persephones.

The boys have watched the river
these past nights and forecast fish.
They've noted times the bailiffs scout
the bridge and banks; they argue gaffs
and spears, the proper lamp—the way
they talk you'd need a winch to haul the trout!

In corners lovers whisper oaths.
Men hold a glass before their mouths
to tell a comment, episodes—
a neighbour's will, a secret spilled,
'He made it most by spending none'.
Mean? 'He'd mind mice at a four crossroads.'

And was he married? 'Not at all, a family
would need feeding.'
                            There's Bill Tuite,
confined to Coca Cola, delighting all with wit
and courtesy; the Trapper Cadden, saying
little, watching all—he dreams of terriers,
of digs at foxes' holes midweek, a freer spirit.

We're watching the Sheridan girls, Ronan
and I, and wondering if she'll appear,
the blackhaired girl from Ballyduff.
There's Jennifer, Louise, Iris—their names
like plants'—and boys preparing invitations,
bold with wishes, risking their rebuff.

44

There's Benny Tobin interspersing all he says
with sayings. 'You've often heard it said,
there are more days nor years, Well now, the way
it is . . .' reminding us 'we'll be a long time
dead, and wouldn't it be worse
if we could not give out the pay

and *céilí* here and there?' And that man
earns the kindest word.
                              The television's loud
though no one looks or listens.
We notice when it's off. We want whatever
isn't there, magnetised by mystery,
and linger after hours, confederate citizens.

Men there all night greet like long-
separated friends, 'Is it yourself?' 'It was
came it.' 'You're well?' 'There's not a bother
on me.' Talk of weather. Then, 'What time is it?'
'What day, you mean.' 'It's time to go,
a woman's waiting, time to get the fother.'

Phil's screaming 'Time' and pulling pints.
'Goodnights' all round. Some order cargoes,
six packs, bottles. There's talk of dances,
discothèques in Kells and Crover, a band
in Virginie . . . an eager hosting slipped
like hounds into the moonlit night, its chances.

Brothers

I hadn't heard a word he said
because he spoke so quietly
and because, the night it was,
we were quiet as nuns in a library.

Four in the morning—
had someone woken and not stirred
from bed we might have passed as cattle
grinding stones along the bank. A word,

a glance could put an end to shadows
in moonlight and lamplight
on water, flickering here, there,
moving upriver. As if by second sight

John Joe went first, walked down the ditch
and worked his way back along the riverbed,
testing the ground. He said little
or nothing, nothing we heard. A spearhead

glistened—he might have been Neptune,
Brittanica on English coins,
or the devil himself, in one hand a trident,
in the other a torch, as he purloins

the world's lost, lazy souls,
but we had salmon and trout
in mind and John Joe never missed. Fish kicked
and bumped along the headland, in the boot

of the car, and tumbled from the scales
as we drank cups of tea
and fumbled with rough cuts of bread.
We talked of nothing else. I'd give them willingly

away but someone's sure to thank you in a pub
standing next or near
a bailiff. We were votaries of darkness.
By this nightwork I witnessed grown men adhere

to their own laws,
crying out *I want to live my life.*
We made a plan and each of them began
his own return to the world and his wife,

to the light of day. There's a way in which
we'll always call each other 'Brother'.
I'm at it still, I'm still in the dark
putting one foot in front of the other.

Winter Work

Friends are unhappy; their long night
finds no day, their lane no turn. They wait
for things to change, as if history
happens to others, elsewhere. They hibernate

in dreams and fear. And Cathryn writes from Dublin:
she lies awake at night and hears
the noise of cars on Rathgar Road,
far from where her life coheres.

I warm to winter work, its rituals
and routines, and find—indoors
and out—a deal of pleasure, alone
or going out to work with neighbours,

a *meitheal* still. All I approve persists,
is here, at home. I think it exquisite
to stand in the yard, my feet on the ground,
in cowshit and horseshit and sheepshit.